"Better Call Saul!"

With thanks to Rob Wijeratna and Joanne Davey at Rocket Licensing Ltd.,
Donna Bruschi and Colleen Stanton at Sony Pictures, and AMC and the producers
and writers of *Breaking Bad*.

BETTER CALL SAUL

HarperCollins books may be purchased for educational, business, or sales promotional use.
For information please email the Special Markets Department at SPsales@harpercollins.com.

Published in 2015 by
Harper Design
An Imprint of HarperCollins*Publishers*
195 Broadway
New York, NY 10007
Tel: (212) 207-7000
Fax: (855) 746-6023
harperdesign@harpercollins.com
www.hc.com

Distributed throughout the world by
HarperCollins*Publishers*
195 Broadway
New York, NY 10007

Commissioning Editor: Lorna Russell
Editor: Elen Jones
Text: David Stubbs
Design: Amazing15 Ltd.
Licensed by Rocket Licensing Ltd.

Library of Congress Control Number: 2014956165
ISBN 978-0-06-240454-1
Printed in the United States

First Printing, 2015

"Better Call Saul!"

THE WORLD ACCORDING TO
SAUL GOODMAN
ATTORNEY AT LAW

HARPER
DESIGN
An Imprint of HarperCollins Publishers

WELCOME L

INTRODUCTION

How does he get away with it? Saul Goodman, that is. Albuquerque's best-known, and dare we say favorite, attorney-at-law. His commercials are low-budget cinematic gems and his website, www.bettercallsaul.com, is a masterpiece of eye-catching tastelessness. Injured at work? Involved in a fender bender? Or maybe a wee homicide? Then you'd better call Saul; the sooner the better if you want to take advantage of his limited-time-only two-for-one misdemeanor shoplifting special. Operating out of one of Albuquerque's finest strip malls, Saul Goodman is the man to see when you need a lawyer with elastic ethics and a cash-operated conscience. He'll bend the law any which way you please, just so long as you can afford his hourly rate.

The law was once seen as a noble pursuit, but Saul is a far cry from Honest Abe Lincoln and the other esteemed attorneys of American history. John Adams? Lawyer. Thomas Jefferson? Lawyer. George Washington? Well, not a lawyer, but he certainly knew a few. The profession's reputation has suffered over the years, muddied by droves of ambulance chasers hawking their services on daytime television. To discover the origins of Saul Goodman and his ilk, we have to go back to the seventies, and the pioneering case of *Bates v. State Bar of Arizona*.

The eponymous John Bates practiced law in Arizona with his partner, Van O'Steen. Instead of charging expensive fees to a handful of clients, they provided legal services at modest rates for routine matters—uncontested divorces, personal bankruptcy cases, and the like. Since the profit margins were smaller, success in their venture depended upon attracting a high volume of clients. In 1976, they placed an ad in a local newspaper to promote their services to the masses and quickly landed in hot water with the State Bar of Arizona. Back then, it was believed that advertising was "unprofessional": lawyers should rely on their well-merited reputations alone.

Bates and O'Steen took the case right up to the Supreme Court, however, who in 1977 decided in their favor. As if the specter of Saul Goodman was yet unfathomable, part of the judgment read, "We suspect that, with advertising, most lawyers will behave as they always have: they will abide by their solemn oaths to uphold the integrity and honor of their profession and of the legal system." Thereafter, the floodgates opened. Bans on lawyers advertising were lifted in state after state, and before the year was out, Jacoby & Meyers became the first law firm in the United States to advertise on television. By the eighties, TV commercials were commonplace, many of them of the "slip and fall" variety—aiming to attract would-be litigants seeking compensation after injuring themselves on the premises of stores and other businesses. The stage was set for Saul Goodman.

WELCOME, LAWBREAKERS!
Saul's Office

his is who he hires?" Walt exclaims with disbelief as he and Jesse pull up outside of Saul's office following Badger's arrest. Maybe it's the neon "Open" sign, reminiscent of a roadside diner, or more likely the inflatable Statue of Liberty on the roof is the concern—but either way, Walt is not impressed. After losing the coin toss with Jesse to make first contact with Saul, Walt enters the reception area posing as Badger's uncle. It's fair to say that Walt's face is conspicuous, even obscured as it is by shades and a lowered baseball cap. As much as when he later witnesses Gus slitting the throat of his own henchman, you can see him reconsidering his life choices as he surveys the waiting room. Screaming babies, a receptionist seated behind bulletproof glass, and Venetian blinds pulled down to keep out both the sunlight and inquiring eyes all contribute to the despondent atmosphere, as does the pitiful collection of Saul's clients. As the inscription on the real Statue of Liberty would describe them: these are the tired, the poor, the huddled masses yearning to breathe free.

THE ONE-STOP SHOP FOR ALL YOUR LEGAL NEEDS!

Once admitted by intercom to the office, Walt's sense of culture shock deepens, even as Saul affably ushers him in to take a seat. From the diploma on the wall to the backdrop of fake pillars and the massive replica of the Constitution behind Saul's desk, there's an air of counterfeit elegance and cut-rate flashiness about the room that isn't entirely reassuring. What's more, the aversion to Albuquerque's abundant natural light is even more noticeable inside Saul's inner sanctum. Instead of windows, he has several high, frosted-glass portholes—the kind you might expect inside an ocean liner. The pallid beige paint on the walls add to an air of seasickness as Walt steps uncertainly aboard the Good Ship Shady, and us with him. Hold on to your stomachs: this is Saul's world.

Inevitably, the ambience brings to mind the shadowy rooms in which the unscrupulous business of the *Godfather* movies was conducted. For all its paper-thin lawyerly embellishments, this space is more like a bunker than an office. The dubiousness of Saul's operation is further emphasized whenever you see the exterior: wedged in between an empty outlet and a Vietnamese restaurant in the center of a desolate strip mall, the parking lot cracked through exposure to the sun's unremitting rays. On the edge of town, on the edge of legality.

Walt's wrinkled nose suggests that with his educated acumen, he's already pegged the lawyer as a fraud. But, as Walt will eventually concede, Saul is nothing if not a shrewd operator. To be able to work as discreetly and effectively as he does from this place, all the while loudly advertising his services with retina-scalding primary colors, attention-seeking TV commercials, and high-visibility inflatable objects, shows that he is a man skilled in the noble art of cunning. Small wonder that, although Walt can never quite shed his disdain at winding up in such questionable surroundings, he returns time and again to this ridiculous (albeit effective!) legal jester in the hope of extricating himself from new jams of his own making.

Saul's Office
FIXTURES
AND FITTINGS

The whole minimalist thing never blew my hair back," remarks Saul upon paying his first visit to Jesse's Spartan accommodations. In terms of the aesthetic approach of his office, Saul opts for just the right amount of bric-a-brac to impress his clientele, most of whom wouldn't know how a reputable law firm is supposed to look. Minimalism would look cheap, and clients want a lawyer who radiates success when they face the possibility of a lengthy prison stay.

With that in mind, Saul chose to pursue a more maximal décor, even if he probably didn't break the bank at the furniture store to come by it. Those chairs Walt and Jesse sit in are certainly leather-backed, but likely acquired from the cheap end of the catalog. Those imposing Grecian pillars are revealed to be quite lightweight when paranoid Saul lifts one, searching his office for electronic bugs. And his phone? That's no one's definition of cutting edge. There are some bound legal volumes visible on his shelves, but they're all for show—Saul is the sort of lawyer who thinks on his feet and lives off his wits instead of going by the book. Granted, Saul's "World's Greatest Lawyer" mug is not the sort of thing an Ivy League alumna would have anywhere near her desk, but it strikes a cozy, good-humored note. What's more, in both its folksiness and the confidence that it projects, the mug impresses those gullible members of the public to take up Saul's services.

Look even closer, and you will see items that hint at a genuine, if gaudy, pride on Saul's behalf of his status as a lawyer. Witness, for example, those miniature, gold-plated scales of justice. Jesse offhandedly uses them as an ashtray, but that doesn't faze Saul. The law is a flexible and versatile thing, and he has tipped the scales himself on more than one occasion.

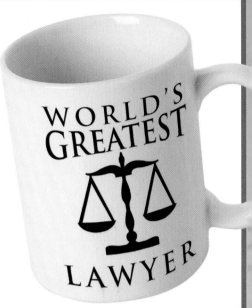

Most important of all are the practical day-to-day tools of the trade, which Saul ensures are stashed close at hand. These include a small bottle of Wite-Out, which (for the benefit of younger readers) was once a vital staple of office stationery in the days before computers and the "delete" button, essential when last-minute corrections needed to be made. Saul's world is all about paper transactions, and not just financial. Computers barely figure. Wite-Out is crucial for making appropriate "amendments."

Then, there are his desk drawers. It's here that he keeps his generous supply of Xanax (for when clients get panicky) and his stash of disposable cell phones (for those who don't want to leave a telecommunications footprint—himself included). In the top drawer, closest at hand: his gun. Readily available for when you've benignly lifted illegal substances from a volatile client's pocket and they haven't taken kindly to the gesture, storming into your office with the intention of punching your lights out.

Finally, there is the couch. It's not a fashionably upholstered settee, but it's plenty comfortable and oft-frequented as a sofa-cum-psychiatrist's couch. As Saul knows all too well, 99 percent of his job is counseling, persuading, charming, deceiving, medicating—all the stuff they don't teach you in law school.

"DID YOU NOT PLAN FOR THIS CONTINGENCY? I MEAN, THE STARSHIP *ENTERPRISE* HAD A SELF-DESTRUCT BUTTON. I'M JUST SAYING."

Saul Goodman

Saul Goodman

LAW-SCHOOL GRADUATE

"**W**here did you get your law degree, Goodman? The same clown college you got that suit?" jeers Hank after Saul's once again extracted a client from a legally questionable interrogation. But Hank's insult has missed its mark, for Saul displays his degree in his office with pride. It's from the University of American Samoa, and it assures all those who read its letters that Saul Goodman is a bona fide law-school graduate, with all the rights, privileges and obligations appertaining thereto. UAS (Go Land Crabs!) might not be near Yale Law in the rankings, but the education provided on those sandy shores in the South Pacific is both affordable and fully accredited.

A quick check with the State Bar of New Mexico would find Saul Goodman to be a lawyer in good standing (let's ignore that rather bulky disciplinary file for the time being—those were all clearly misunderstandings). Much as Bugs Bunny (and perhaps *Breaking Bad*!) put Albuquerque on the map, Saul is surely UAS's most famous alumnus. Move over, canned tuna, American Samoa has a new chief export.

COMFORTABLE IN MY WINGTIPS
Saul's Attire

Were he a man of thinner skin, that crack Hank made about his clownish attire would have wounded Saul as much as the slight about his degree, for Saul is a man who thinks very carefully about his ensemble. While it may look as if he acquired most of his wardrobe at a clearance sale back in 1989, there's no denying that the fellow is dapper to a fault. No somber gravitas for him—he's not running a funeral parlor. Instead, he goes for an electric array of colors, from golds and greens to purples and reds, the sort of colors that come affably at you like a guy who says hello with finger guns.

6000 MENSWEAR

HALF OFF
ALL SUITS

LOOK SHARP FOR YOUR DAY IN COURT

Discount suits for all clients of Saul Goodman

BETTERCALLSAUL.COM

When we first meet Saul, he's decked out relatively conservatively: dark brown pinstripe suit, candy-striped tie, and crisp pocket handkerchief—not yet the full eyeful. However, that gold lapel pin with the scales of justice is a permanent fixture. As he becomes further embroiled in Walt's schemes, his wardrobe begins to clash severely—turquoise shirt battling with a purple tie that's run through with a collar pin nearing the size of a railroad spike, with the added feature of a Wayfarer 515 ribbon worn in ostentatious tribute to the victims of the tragic mid-air plane collision. Even if he didn't say a word, Saul would still be the loudest person in the room.

Some time later, as he and Jesse stand at yet another meeting in the desert, Saul's cumulative color scheme of yellow, gold, purple, and blue looks as increasingly overwhelmed as he is. The clown colors are no longer hacking it. As his world begins to unravel, we begin to catch sight of his off-hours looks: a velour track suit here, a retro white jacket, and open-neck red T-shirt there.

Finally, as he goes into the underworld equivalent of the Witness Protection Program, he's down to just a purple shirt and slacks. The last we see of him, he's wearing a simple white shirt, facing a future in which he's "Mr. Low Profile—just another douchebag with a job and three pairs of Dockers." Does this tell us that the stylish outfits were purely for business, rather than personal pride or vanity? Yes, and now it indicates that he's been thoroughly drained of his Saul persona. The suits, the shirts, and the ties weren't just the outward signs of a sweet-talking, two-bit lawyer; they were also the expression of a boundlessly optimistic, opportunistic, problem-solving personality. Saul in chinos managing a Cinnabon in Omaha? Unthinkable. Saul Goodman will always find a way to bounce back, likely with a wardrobe full of yesteryear's best threads close at hand.

TAKE A LOAD OFF

Saul's Relaxation Techniques

Take off your shoes, lay back, exfoliate," says Saul as he invites Jesse into a nail salon, recommending the "full treatment." He's also recommending that his young client launder his drug money through the salon, but why not strike two birds with one stone and indulge in some genuine rest and recuperation? Saul doesn't go so far as to undo his top shirt button or loosen his tie, but his shoes and socks are off and a few strands of hair have fallen across his eyebrow, indicating that this is about as relaxed as Saul gets, his fingers and toes enjoying a methodic buffing from the salon's female staff. He's not like Walt, who used a rare free moment to unwind by compulsively removing dry rot from his home with a frenzied zeal that put his family on edge—or Jesse, who invited a few dozen friends and strangers to his house for loud music, uncut pizza, and nearly a week of non-stop, nihilistic partying.

Natural Nail Spa
and Boutique

NAIL SPA

tel. 464

beauty salon

Come and live a
lifestyle experience

Yo

SPA TREATMENTS
Beauty and Pampering

Manicures, pedicures, waxing treatments and more...
let our hands do the work.

Well
& Beauty

Saul is a man of gentler vices. We know he keeps plenty of Xanax in stock—a drug commonly used to treat anxiety and panic disorders, which can easily develop when you've got Walter White for a client. However, even better than the chemical options are the pampering pleasures of the massage parlor and the nail salon. A car wash? Without the added benefit of lovely women gently massaging the customer with chamois leathers in the comfort of a reclining seat, where's the fun in that?

Saul also enjoys stretching out in his chi machine, catching whatever opportunity he can to let it work gently over those lower back muscles, so apt to clamp up, wobbling and jiggling with quiet ecstasy as he takes yet another frantic call from Walt. If possible, however, he prefers the old-fashioned treatment of a human hand—preferably female. On one such occasion, Jesse bursts into Saul's office just as he is buttoning up his green shirt following an office massage. "Barn door open," notes the Vietnamese masseuse contemptuously, eyeing his trousers. One hopes that Saul isn't wholly dependent on these sessions for…satisfaction.

"THERE ARE RULES TO THIS LAWYER THING"

Saul's Ethics

Did you actually just use the word 'ethically' in a sentence? You're not Clarence Darrow, Saul. You're a two-bit, bus-bench lawyer." So jeers Walt, as Saul delicately explains to him how he was obliged, out of lawyer-client confidentiality, to conceal from Walt the scheme he arranged with Walt's wife Skyler to give away a large sum of his money in order to pay off her former boss and ex-lover Ted's tax bill. "She's my client—same as you…I try my best, ethically."

It's tempting to share Walt's incredulity. A man who casually brings up the option of murder during business meetings, who launders money with the same everyday nonchalance that most men would launder their underwear, whose Rolodex contains contact numbers for some of the shadiest criminal operators north of the Mexican border…this is a man who can claim to be trying his best, ethically?

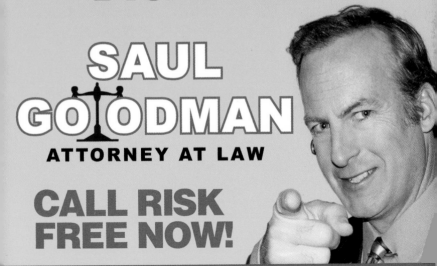

Well, strangely, yes. If there is one area in which Saul has a shred of scruples, it's in his determination to maintain the lawyerly ethics he swore to uphold upon joining the state bar. There are certain lines he will not cross. Well, maybe he'll cross them if you put a gun to his head, but even then there's some wiggle room when you've got a brain like Saul's. So it is when Mike bursts in on Saul and demands to know Jesse's whereabouts, needing to have a not-so-friendly chat with the young man. Saul is reluctant to give Jesse up, and explains that this would be in violation of his legal principles— even when Mike proposes that he beat Saul until his legs don't work. "If I were to tell you, I just wouldn't be able to live with myself," Saul protests.

However, when Mike prepares to launch into the assault, Saul swiftly offers that he may have written down Jesse's location nearby—for his own reference, of course. A quick perusal of his desk might turn up a notepad with Jesse's current whereabouts, a trailer park in the state of Virginia. On the surface, it looks as if Saul has sold out a client in peril, but in truth Jesse is still in New Mexico, safely ensconced in Saul's favorite abandoned laser-tag arena. Even when his life is in mortal danger, only two things are on his mind: talking his way out of a jam and preserving the niceties that allow him to look himself in the mirror in the morning and say to himself that whatever else he is, he is Saul Goodman, Attorney-at-Law. There are, as he puts it to Mike, "rules to this lawyer thing," and he is determined to abide by them.

We also see this during one of his first encounters with Walt and Jesse, who abduct him in ski masks and kneel him in front of a freshly dug grave in order to persuade him to accept $10,000 to help out on Badger's case—on the condition that he doesn't cut a deal with Badger to rat them out to the DEA. Still trembling with terror, Saul's problem-solving mind quickly arrives at a solution. "Why don't you just kill Badger?" As he slowly realizes he's dealing with a pair of hapless fledglings, he decides to go into business with them. Even as his hands are tied, he insists that they put a dollar in his jacket pocket as a retainer to establish attorney-client privilege: their secrets will be safe with him, "under threat of disbarment." Kill Badger, don't kill Badger, whatever...but some things are sacred.

"YEAH, YOU DO SEEM TO HAVE A LITTLE SHIT-CREEK ACTION GOING... YOU KNOW, FYI, YOU CAN BUY A PADDLE."

Saul Goodman

"MY A-TEAM"

Saul's Associates

Saul Goodman and Associates" reads the sign, implying that he leads a team of lawyers whisked straight from their Harvard graduation ceremonies to Saul's strip-mall office. In fact, his "associates" include his mammoth bodyguard, Huell; his "carrottop" henchman, Kuby; and Francesca, his imposing receptionist.

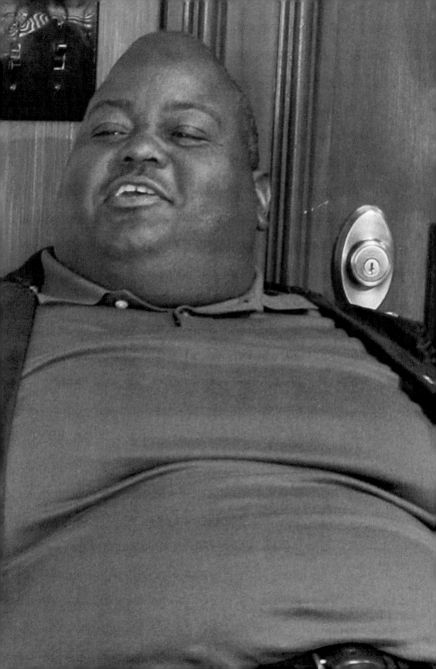

When Walt's troubles endanger Saul, the cagey lawyer finds the largest bodyguard in the Southwest and plants him in the lobby. An intimidating presence to be sure, Huell is like a mountain in both size and speed. He might enjoy the occasional nap while on the clock, and he may interrupt important conferences to relieve his bladder, but there is magic in Huell's "fingers the size of hot dogs." He can bypass locks with ease, and more notably, Huell is a pickpocket of dazzling skill (see box).

To see Huell fatefully lift a baggie of marijuana from Jesse's pocket as he leaves Saul's office in the Season Five episode "Confessions" requires extensive and repeated use of the slow rewind and freeze-frame button. Sadly, the last we see of him is two episodes later, left in a room "for his own protection" and told not to move until DEA agents Hank and Gomez come back, which, sadly, they never do. He's presumably still in that room now.

If verbal finesse is called for, Saul turns to Kuby, a Boston-bred criminal who moved out west for the sunshine after things got too hot in Beantown. His skills are on display when he poses as a hazardous-waste official to ease Walt's purchase of the car wash, though that credit must be shared with Skyler, who feeds him technical jargon through an earpiece.

Kuby and Huell are the Rosencrantz and Guildenstern of this story— peripheral observers rather than main players. When they're sent to fetch Walt's gigantic stockpile of money, they know they'll never personally get to spend it—but at least they're able to have some fun lying on the cash like it's a giant mattress, fantasizing about running away to Mexico. As a working duo, they're not always effective—though it's not really their fault that when they try to intimidate Ted, Skyler's hapless tax-dodging boss, as he tries to flee, he trips on a loose rug and hits his head, landing himself in a coma. "Act of God," Huell explains to Saul. "No accounting for an act of God."

Most formidable of Saul's associates is Francesca, who has as few scruples as her boss. When Hank corners Walt and Jesse inside their mobile meth-lab RV, they reach out to Saul for help—and Francesca obliges, calling Hank under the guise of a hospital worker and informing him that his wife has been in a serious accident. Justly, she demands a raise after performing this service. Perhaps her finest moment involves facing down Walt after he breaks into missing-in-action Saul's office. "Let me explain something to you," Walt says. "My partner and I—" "Are in danger? Whoopty-freaking-doo!" she mocks, having had a bellyful of the endless perils that are Walt's stock-in-trade. "How's that news, exactly—you two being in danger? After doing something idiotic?"

Finally, she demands payment for the broken office door. He offers $1,700. She demands $20,000. Walt sputters that "no reputable vendor" would demand such a sum, at which point she coolly ups the price to $25,000 before it finally clicks with Walt that this is the price for Saul's number, not the door. Walter White—killer of Gus Fring, drug kingpin, the legendary Heisenberg himself—is no match for a pissed-off receptionist. This is her severance package, and she more than deserves it.

SMOOTH CRIMINAL

"**You don't want a criminal lawyer—you want a *criminal lawyer.*"** Saul would be deeply flattered if he had heard Jesse describe him thus to Walt. Despite the folksy image he projects to the kindhearted would-be litigants of Albuquerque, behind closed doors Saul doesn't shy away from the fact that he is an honest-to-goodness criminal lawyer, at your service.

Saul doesn't flinch or adopt a more sinister persona when discussing nefarious matters: he smoothly exudes criminal knowledge the same way he pitches legitimate legal advice in his commercials. If you want someone to go that extra mile into the downright felonious, then Saul is your man, as long as he doesn't go from defender to defendant as a result. He's not dumb—when Skyler mentions Walt's meth lab in conversation to him during a phone call, he's forced to pretend they have a bad connection: "Whoa! You're breaking up there!" But otherwise, Saul is as proud to be a friend of the sinner as he is of his tie collection. When you need someone to pull your chestnuts out of the fire, to keep you from crossing that fine line between criminal and convict—better call Saul!

FROM PARKING TICKETS TO MASS MURDER
Saul's Clientele

Who then, are the people filling Saul's waiting room, beside whom Walt must sit while he awaits an audience? These are society's low fliers, the hopeful dregs of the American citizenry, humble folk in search of Kentucky Fried Justice. Over there sits a menacing-looking fellow in a neck brace, clearly looking to make a dubious "slip and fall" compensation claim, while next to him a small boy picks his nose, and across the room a muscle-bound man paces back and forth. On later visits, Walt must endure being stared at fondly by a large lady in denim as Skyler sits to his left, opposite a woman with a permanent hacking cough for which she may or may not be seeking legal remedy.

What has attracted them to Saul's office? His commercials, of course. Traffic accident? Injured on the job? Committed mass murder? What are you waiting for? Practically every misdemeanor and felony is catered to by Saul, the friend of (alleged) perpetrator and victim alike. He will not judge you: no matter your style or odor, no matter how high the probability that you did the deed or how low the probability that you're a genuine victim of anything other than your own greed.

If you're willing to be economical with the truth, and you brought along a cashier's check, Saul will certainly assist you along shady paths—as we see when he solicitously asks a seemingly injured client if his neck brace is causing him any distress. "It's tight," complains the accident victim as his dear old mother looks on, adding that he's having difficulty breathing. "Need you breathing," says Saul, producing a crate full of alternative neck braces, one of which fits better, before ushering them out the door, addressing his parting remarks to the mother, who no doubt came up with the idea of having her son pay Saul a visit in the first place.

With litigation now no longer the sole prerogative of those with money to burn on big-shot lawyers, the opportunities for lawsuits are endless. Saul lists the extensive and bewildering array on his website. The potential targets of a lawsuit range from financial institutions and employers to realtors, suppliers, glassblowers, companies from other countries that made the drugs that were turned into the drugs you took, Amish elders, even yourself.

Saul's waiting room, admittedly, is a hellish parlor of human desperation. But Walt should not regard its inhabitants too contemptuously. The truth is, he's much worse than them. Their crimes and deceits are, like their fees, penny-ante compared to his.

Saul may be many things, but he's no snob: he welcomes all his clients with a smile and a handshake. His waiting room may be chaotic, but from chaos comes the opportunity for profit.

"I'M NO VITO CORLEONE."
Walter H. White

"NO SHIT! RIGHT NOW
YOU'RE FREDO!"
Saul Goodman

IT'S ALL GOOD, MAN
Saul's Name

Among the first things we learn about Saul Goodman is that his name isn't actually "Saul Goodman." But then again, neither is Walt's last name really "Mayhew," the pseudonym he somewhat unconvincingly poses under when he first meets the lawyer who will become his not-altogether-trusted right-hand man. "Faith and begorrah—a fellow potato eater!" declares Saul, disclosing that he himself is actually of Irish descent, even if you wouldn't know it from that accent. His name, he reveals, is McGill. "The Jew thing I just do for the homeboys—they all want a pipe-hittin' member of the tribe, so to speak."

While clearly a promotional tool, Saul's willingness to shed his given name and take up a new one gives us a peek into his psyche. Unlike Walt, who is as flexible as a solid oak, Saul is a palm tree bending in the wind. He is, at his core, a survivor. If one identity trips him up, he can leave it behind without dwelling on the philosophical ramifications. Saul never has to ask himself "Who am I?" because regardless of the name on his business cards, it's all good, man.

AN AMERICAN HERO
Saul the Patriot

I f there's one thing Saul knows about his business, it's that in America, it's impossible to be too patriotic, especially when you are trying to convince the public that you're the man to trust with their hard-earned dollars. The whole sordid enterprise of extracting money from large companies on the basis of bogus personal injuries takes on a more noble air when it is presented as your solemn duty as an American citizen.

Patriotism plays great on TV, and the thicker and more shamelessly you apply it, the better. It's the note first struck as you approach Saul's office—that inflatable Statue of Liberty flapping proudly in the desert breeze; that red, white, and blue signage—and it continues as you enter into the reception area and notice that the mood Muzak is something along the lines of the stirring "America the Beautiful." And then, of course, it hits you squarely between the eyes when you finally get an audience with Saul Goodman himself, flanked by that gigantic wall print of the United States' Constitution. This is what it's all about in the good ol' US of A: life, liberty and the pursuit of the almighty dollar.

"OH MY GOD! YOU REALLY ARE A CHEMISTRY TEACHER! HEH-HEH...I WAS TERRIBLE AT CHEMISTRY. I'M MORE OF A HUMANITIES GUY."

Saul Goodman

"I FIGHT FOR YOU, ALBUQUERQUE!"

It's always a desert," groans Saul as he waits patiently in the middle-of-nowhere sandy wasteland with Jesse. He looks utterly overdressed for the rugged New Mexico terrain, where cargo shorts and hiking boots would be the more appropriate attire. Saul, of course, could never bring himself to wear that to work. He would no more willingly remove his suit than a knight would his armor. So what's he doing here, this city-slicker type? Why isn't he working out of Chicago or Boston or New York, among his own sort? What on earth brings him all the way down to Albuquerque?

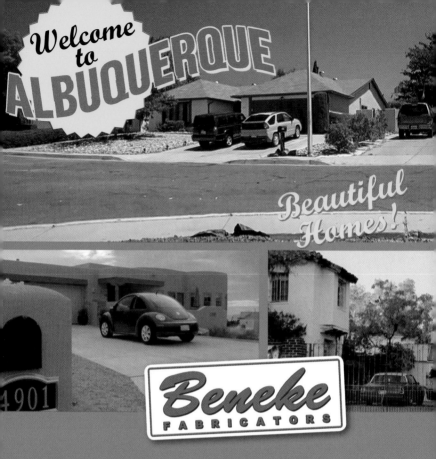

Beautiful Homes!

Well, for a start, the easy pickings. Saul would be one of a thousand lawyers in the urban metropolises of America. Down here in Albuquerque, however, he is the big fish in a small pond. With his shamelessly jazzy spiel, Saul can attract all the Stars and Stripes–revering folk who have been persuaded that it's part of their American birthright to get whatever's coming to them from those big-city institutions, and he doesn't have to compete for their attention.

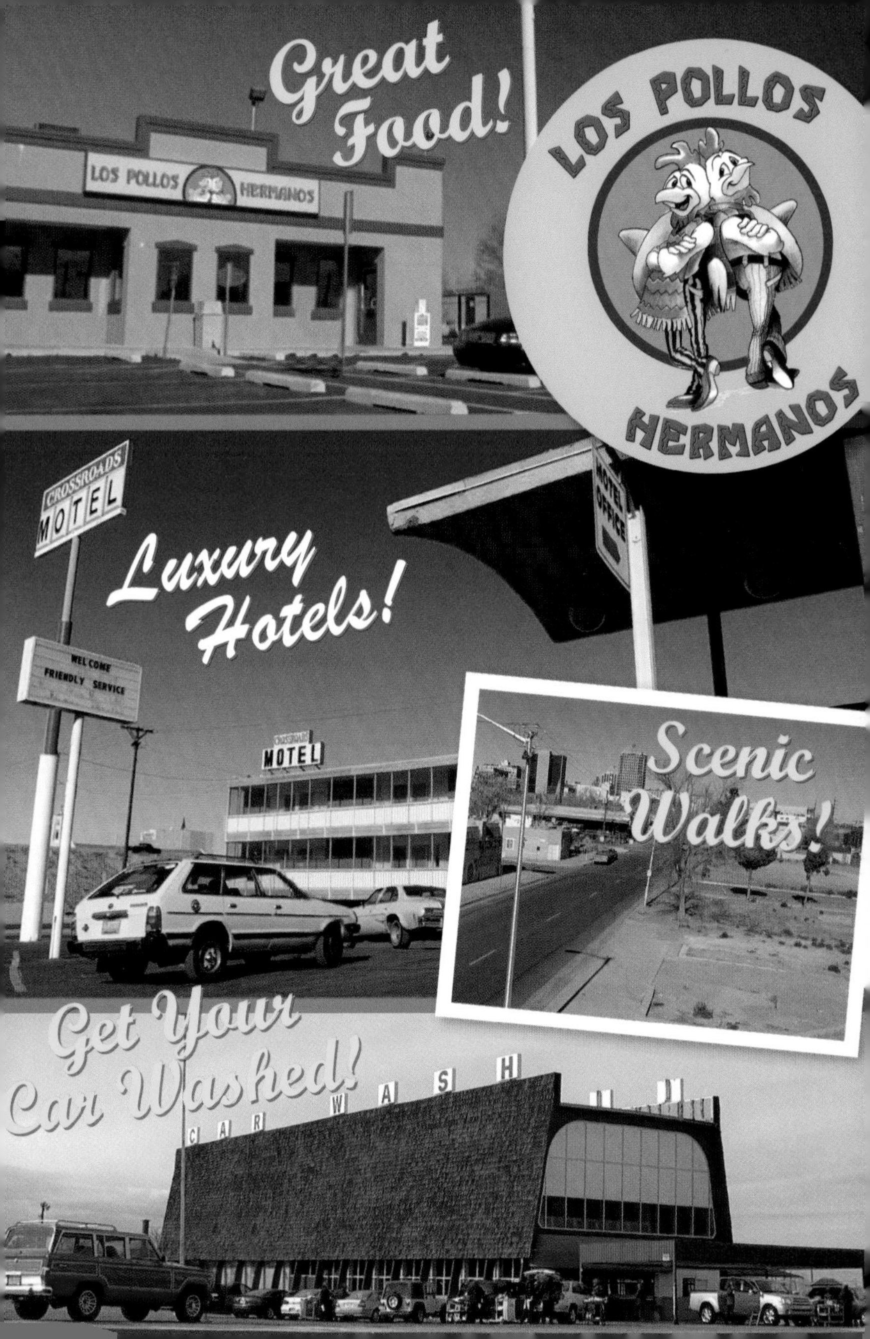

Great Food!

LOS POLLOS HERMANOS

LOS POLLOS HERMANOS

CROSSROADS MOTEL

MOTEL OFFICE

Luxury Hotels!

WELCOME
FRIENDLY SERVICE

CROSSROADS
MOTEL

Scenic Walks!

Get Your Car Washed!

CAR WASH

Luxury Living!

Thriving Businesses!

Great Camping!

VAMONOS
PEST

And then, there is the location of the city itself, situated in the heart of the Wild West. It is here that Saul the criminal as well as criminal lawyer finds himself well-established with a healthy client base. If America is the land of opportunity, then Albuquerque is particularly fertile territory, despite its arid landscapes. There are bodies and booty buried out in those there hills, which are the perfect setting for all manner of criminal doings—not to mention that the proximity to the Mexican border provides a healthy flow of illegal narcotics and the legal mayhem that follows close behind.

Saul might moan about the desert, especially as he has come within an inch of being buried there himself, but he of all people should realize that he owes his living to this godforsaken place.

Of course, the multiple murders that take place in *Breaking Bad*'s fictionalized Albuquerque, thanks largely to one disgruntled chemistry teacher, distort reality. The city's homicide rate is about on par with that of Los Angeles, much lower than Detroit, Chicago, or even glitzy Miami. Where the city distinguishes itself is in property crimes, with double the rate of LA and triple the rate of New York City. Its annual crimes against people and property alone total more than 33,000 among a population of 555,000, meaning each resident has a one-in-nineteen chance of being a victim. Excellent for Saul, of course: perpetrators of crime as well as victims of accident are his specialty.

SAUL GOES DOWN 1
Walter

When Walt discovers that Skyler has been having an affair with her boss, his temper gets the better of him and he heads to Beneke Fabricators to confront her lover Ted himself. Luckily, Saul has bugged the White house, and sends Mike to pick Walt up before he gets into more trouble. Afterward, Saul commiserates with Walt's lady troubles, "Sure, she snuck off the reservation to get some dirty, damp, and deep, but—"POW. Haven't you been watching the body language, Saul? Walt's not in the mood—though it's not clear whether Skyler's dalliance or Saul's surveillance is a bigger offense to his ego.

SAUL GOES DOWN 2
Jesse

When Jesse realizes that it was Walt, not meth kingpin Gus Fring, that poisoned his girlfriend's eight-year-old son, he's beyond furious. This rage extends to Saul—who was complicit in Walt's plan to manipulate Jesse with the help of his bodyguard's sticky fingers. It's a shame that Huell isn't as skillful a bodyguard as he is a pickpocket. "What do I pay you for?!" he seethes at his personal defender after Jesse pummels Saul in his own office.

"I KNOW A GUY"
Saul's Connections

Let's just say I may know a guy who knows a guy. Who knows another guy."

Whatever your criminal needs, the solution is only a couple of phone calls away for Saul Goodman. Need someone to take a sudden (and permanent) vacation to Belize? Saul knows a couple of guys west of the Rockies who are discreet masters in the art of whacking. Or maybe you'd like a Rolex or diamond ring on the cheap? Saul's man Ira has bargains you wouldn't believe. No need to charge full price when you've "acquired" it for free.

If murder or jewelry is not the answer to your particular conundrum, don't worry: Saul's Rolodex contains all sorts of hidden gems. He has a lady in Tax and Revenue, in case you need to take a peek at anyone's books, and "Jimmy In-n-Out" provides an even more specialized service. The outside world has not been too kind to Jimmy, so for a price, he'll go to prison for you. Of course, the lion's share of that fee goes to Saul. "For facilitating," Saul explains. "Who's taking the bigger risk here? Jimmy likes prison!"

Then there's Mike Ehrmantraut, who Saul hires to perform bugging and "cleaning" services, among other things (not unlike Harvey Keitel's Wolf in *Pulp Fiction*). Despite leaving the Philadelphia PD under an obscure cloud, this grizzly, nerveless private investigator still has his cop smarts intact, and he can take down guys half his age in twos and threes in a gunfight. Initially, he looks like he might be one of Saul's hired hands—which, technically, he is. Pretty soon, though, it becomes clear that the

chain of command doesn't work that way. When Mike needs information from Saul, he doesn't wait his turn in the reception area—"You're good right there!" Mike tells Saul menacingly as he attempts to get up from a recumbent position on the floor of his office, his legs still being massaged by his chi machine.

Ultimately, Mike answers to a higher power than our beloved attorney-at-law: Gustavo Fring, who puts the fear of God into Saul the same as anyone else. "My name doesn't come up in those meetings?" he gulps, when Walt is discussing the latest round of mortal danger he faces from the friendly fried-chicken franchiser and ruthless drug lord. Finally, when Saul realizes his own day has come—"When they start to whack the lawyers, that's when I draw the line"—he himself must put in a call, on his own behalf as well as Walt's, to the man simply known as the Disappearer, a guy who runs a seemingly innocuous vacuum-repair shop.

For a large fee and at short notice, he will arrange for you to assume a new identity when your life of dalliances with homicidal drug dealers has become a bit too exciting for comfort. He's the last guy you know that you actually want to get in touch with—when you climb into the back of his van, it means the jig is up and your adventures are over. It's a wonder Saul went so long without needing the Disappearer's services, since we know he had dealings with the Mexican cartel even before Walt and Jesse turned his life upside-down.

One thing about the guys Saul knows: they're dangerous guys—strong and silent types (unlike the motor-mouthed Saul), guys who know how to command a room. So does Saul, in his own way, but next to the Disappearer, next to Mike, he visibly shrinks in awe. He may know the guys, but he could never be those guys.

MONEY THAT SPENDS

Saul's Guide to Money Laundering

What good's money that doesn't spend? If a tree falls in the forest...well, you get the point." In such Zen-like terms does Saul express the profound sadness that follows when hard-earned mounds of cash—the sort you have to count by weighing it—can't be spent freely for fear of raising suspicion. It seems so unfair. Walt shares that sense of grievance, unable to take credit for his financial successes while concealing his meth enterprise from his family, and so he must suffer the indignity of having his teenage son set up a website on his behalf, www.savewalterwhite.com, to help fund his ongoing cancer treatments.

In order to keep Skyler and Junior in the dark about Walt's new career, Saul must find a way to "launder" Walt's profits. A bequest from a long-lost relative? "Many are the happy memories of Uncle Murray bouncing me on his knee. We lost track of the old pervert over the years…but, what do ya know? He kicked it and left me millions!" Unacceptable to proud Walt. But, fear not, Saul has the answer to fool both Skyler and the taxman: not a single anonymous benefactor, but benefactors, plural—small donations

Walter White
Father, Husband & Teacher

What a wonderful dad I have,
But he is in trouble.

It's Lung Cancer.
He needs an operation. Now!

To help, please send your contribution
to our operation fund
and keep my Dad in your prayers!

Save Walter White
You can help us raise money for Walt's surgery

**Click Here
to Donate**

channeled from computers around the world as Junior's site goes mysteriously viral. "Mr. Walter H. White! Cancer saint! I'm getting a warm and fuzzy feeling just thinking about it." It helps once again that Saul knows a guy who knows a guy, this time a computer hacker who lives with his mother in Belarus, "so good luck extraditing his fat Russian ass." His trick is to turn strangers' desktop computers into servants that do his bidding, creating the impression that the kind-hearted people of the world have rallied by the thousand to raise funds for Walt, tiny doses that add up to a huge sum. It's exquisite.

If you don't have terminal cancer or some other sympathy-inducing ailment (and let's knock on wood that you don't!), Saul can provide alternate explanations for your sudden windfall. Skyler may have come up with the Walt's-a-blackjack-genius cover story, but Saul made it IRS-proof. "I generate false Currency Transaction Reports out the wazoo, plus all the necessary W-2Gs," he tells the Whites. "I know a couple of casino managers ready to jump at the chance to report false losses. A win-win for everyone."

But for the bigger jobs, you need ideas the size of those giant industrial laundry machines they use to wash comforters. When Saul tries to convince skeptical Jesse that a nail salon is "the best money laundry a growing boy could ask for," he finds his client sullenly reluctant. Thinking that Jesse just doesn't properly understand the mathematics, Saul demonstrates the time-honored and very necessary principle of laundering using cotton balls. Do what you like, but if you party hard with no visible means of income, the IRS will get you like they got Capone. So, here's where the cotton balls come in. "You give me your money, that's called placement." A jar of cotton swabs is the revenue from the nail salon. Add the drug-money cotton balls to the cotton swabs, and you have what's called integration. "And there you have it—nice, clean, taxable income."

There are other, more complicated ways Saul can launder your profits—"Structured deposits, loan-backs, buy-backs, currency exchanges"—but whatever the method, you can depend on him to turn your dirty cash into money that spends.

Advertisement

ILLEGAL TIGER POSSESSION

The meter-reader came by and was mauled by Fluffy?!?

"Better Call Saul!"

Repeat this key phrase:

THAT'S NOT MY TIGER!

Where did it come from?

THE ZOO!

(and you can bet we're gonna sue the bars off them)

What were you doing buying 80lbs of raw meat every week?

THE ATKINS DIET!

Then get that fluffy critter to Texas, because ...

TIGERS = LEGAL IN TEXAS!

(Yeehaw!)

If a tiger's got you by the tail (legally)

BETTERCALLSAUL.COM

Sample case only - not actual legal advice. Saul Goodman Associates and Ice Station Zebra Associates not responsible for consequences of any action present or future - do not lie to law-enforcement entities.

"WHAT IS ICE STATION ZEBRA ASSOCIATES?"

For "totally legit" tax purposes, which need not concern the client or for that matter the IRS, Saul asks that all payments for his services be made out to Ice Station Zebra Associates, a loan-out corporation he has set up to handle all his financial transactions. Loan-out corporations are separate legal entities usually set up by showbiz types such as singers and actors, but for a showman like Saul, they're a natural option.

The logo Ice Station Zebra Associates also appears in small print in his TV commercials. Why not a more bland and discreet moniker? It betrays Saul's taste for the eclectic and cinematic that he would name his company after the 1968 Cold War thriller starring Rock Hudson.

Maybe that's the sort of flourish that impresses those clients who like their lawyers a little slick and slippery? Unfortunately, it backfires on him when Skyler finds a suspicious check in this name and decides to take a more active role in her husband's financial affairs, making Saul's life just a little bit more complicated.

"SOME PEOPLE ARE IMMUNE TO GOOD ADVICE."

Saul Goodman

SAUL THE RAKE

For such a smooth operator, so adept at manipulating clientele and associates alike, Saul does seem to have trouble with women. The colorful—often classless—antics that so endear him to the criminal element are ill-suited for relationships. Saul has successfully wooed women in the past, but it's keeping them around that's the problem. He once convinced a woman that he was Kevin Costner ("It worked because *I* believed it."). However, it's doubtful the ruse lasted long after sunrise. Saul's also been married at least twice. We know little about the first try, but it's likely that relations with his second wife broke down rather quickly after Saul caught her in bed with his own stepfather. Perhaps the older gentleman convinced her that he was Robert Redford?

"CLEARLY HIS TASTE IN WOMEN IS THE SAME AS HIS TASTE IN LAWYERS: ONLY THE VERY BEST...WITH JUST A RIGHT AMOUNT OF DIRTY!"

Saul Goodman

The only constant female in his life is his receptionist, Francesca, but any romantic longings in that dynamic are strictly one-sided. After Francesca pointedly rejects Saul's offer to follow her home "for safety," he watches her walk away and groans, "God, you are killing me with that booty." He'd doubtless have more success if he refrained from vulgar comments like that or from referring to her as "Honey Tits." He insists that it's endearing, but she replies, "You'd better stop calling me that, or I'm going to hang you by your tie." And she would. She's way, way out of his league.

It's hard to know where Saul's courtship troubles originated, but they're nothing new. As he reminisces to Brock: "I loved school—seesaws, story time, chasing girls with sticks..." Perhaps Saul is more suited to abstract relationships, like his longtime dalliance with Lady Justice. It's fitting that Justice is blind, as we're not sure how'd she feel about Saul's flamboyant taste in attire.

"WE HAVE A WIFE PROBLEM"

I guess that's why gangsters have molls," reflects Saul as Walt pours out his woes about keeping his wife in the dark regarding his double life. "Haven't you ever seen *White Heat*," he asks Walt, referring to the 1949 film noir starring James Cagney. "I've seen *White Heat*, but I don't see how that pertains," retorts Walt, with typical salt. Saul very much sees how it pertains. Cagney's wife in the film, played by Virginia Mayo, betrays him and murders his mother. Maybe, Saul offers, you need a moll more than you need a wife whom you can't trust with your secrets.

That's not to be, and when Skyler eventually does become a party to Walt's business, Saul decides that the best foot forward is to lay his charms on her. "Clearly, [Walt's] taste in women is the same as his taste in lawyers: only the very best, with just the right amount of dirty." Finding this line as well-received as an attorney at the Pearly Gates, Saul is forced to clarify, "It's funny, because you're clearly so very classy."

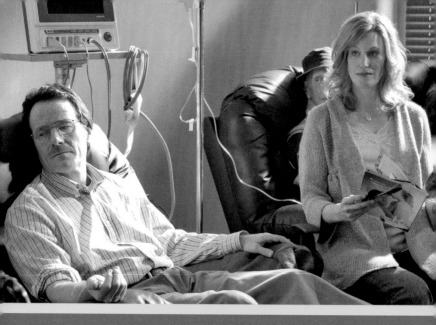

Saul pigeonholes Skyler as a woman blessed with more than her fair share of beauty, but perhaps lacking when it comes to brains. His mistake is dragged into the light when he attempts to explain to her the principles of money laundering as he did with Jesse, this time using a jar of jellybeans for illustration. But Skyler is no Jesse. She politely, but firmly, informs him that she is a bookkeeper and quite familiar with the ins and outs of money laundering.

Walt admits that the idea of faking the story about gambling winnings to account for his newfound financial success was actually Skyler's, and Saul extends another poorly aimed compliment: "You grow more gorgeous by the minute." His flattery soon turns to frustration, however, as she questions the soundness of his plan for Walt to launder his money through a laser-tag facility. "It doesn't add up," says Skyler, ever the bookkeeper. "Scientists love lasers!" Saul replies, trying to hide his agitation. His feelings become quite clear when he brusquely concludes the meeting: "Let me bottom line this for you. You don't need to be involved. I've been doing this successfully for a lot of years—and, believe it or not, without your help!"

What's most interesting is the way he and Skyler have become the angry Mommy and Daddy in this scene, while the ever-prideful Walt rocks in his chair, seething with frustration that he has been cut out of the conversation, like a teenage child at a parent-teacher meeting. Later, when Walt argues that they should use the car wash to launder funds, Saul sneers, "Is that you talking, or Yoko Ono?" This barb lays bare Saul's

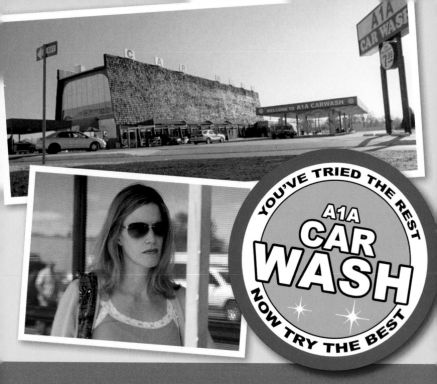

insecurity. He fears that Skyler will break up his lucrative band or—at the very least—make him redundant. Saul's desire has always been to be the Tom Hagen to Walt's Vito Corleone, providing the Godfather with sage advice and taking a healthy percentage of the proceeds.

Eventually, he and Skyler learn to work together, but Saul never fully understands Walt's attachment. How could he, when his own attempts at matrimony fared so poorly? When it looks like Skyler is going to leave Walt, Saul completely misreads his state of mind and says, "There are other fish in the sea. You'd be amazed at what's out there—Thailand, Czech Republic…" Life would be so much easier, albeit a whole lot sleazier, if things were done Saul's way.

"IF YOU'RE NOT WILLING TO
PULL THE TRIGGER ON THIS,
I AM MORE THAN HAPPY TO
CALL GOODMAN MYSELF."

Skyler White

"I GET THAT ALL THE TIME"
Saul the Local Celebrity

The stars shine brightly in the desert skies over Albuquerque, but they pale in comparison to the city's most luminous celestial body: Saul Goodman, Attorney-at-Law. When he visits Skyler at the car wash, she grouses that he's too recognizable. "Your face is plastered on every bus bench in a five-mile radius." "Celebrities get their cars washed just like everybody else," Saul counters. And that's just what Saul is: a local celebrity fueled by ads on bus benches, billboards, and late-night television commercials. With his trademark hair, outfits, and catch phrase, Saul is Bernalillo County's Elvis, and his admirers are not limited to the city's seedy underbelly. Even Skyler's own son is a fan. Upon sighting him, Junior openly gawks at Saul, staring slack-jawed as if the king of rock and roll himself rose from the dead. "I like your commercials," he manages, shyly. Even Jesse's buttoned-up parents recognize Saul, although he misinterprets their dismay at his presence as fascination. He strikes a pose and gives them his famous "Better call Saul!" Then lets them know they shouldn't feel bad about feeling starstruck: "I get that all the time."

Saul and the Police

aul loves nothing better than dealing with the police. He can really relax and be himself down at the station, even though in the outside world he's eventually forced to wear a bulletproof vest for protection. In his own office, he's not entirely safe from threats or physical harm, not with his bodyguard Huell's slow reflexes. No, give him the police every time. It's the one place where he can swagger about knowing he has full, watertight protection from any cop who doesn't want to be slapped with a lawsuit. And, boy, does Saul take advantage of this, letting his loose tongue run free as he evicts law enforcers of all ranks from the interrogation room so that he can have a discreet word alone with his clients.

"ANYTHING YOU CARE TO SHARE WITH ME?"
Saul Goodman

"SURE. YOUR COMMERCIALS? THEY SUCK ASS. I'VE SEEN BETTER ACTING IN AN EPILEPTIC WHORE HOUSE."
Hank Schrader

Indeed, this is how we see him for the very first time, bursting in to protect a nervous and recently arrested Badger from blurting anything so unhelpful as the truth. "What did you say to Babyface, huh? Did you say anything stupid? By anything stupid, I mean anything at all." He then turns his attention to the baby-faced detective, who successfully posed as an addict to entrap Badger—"What? The academy hire you right out of the womb?"—before shooing him away, the poor detective having no choice but to do as he says. "You, out! Ten minutes ago. Go on. There are laws, detective—have your kindergarten teacher read them to you. Go grab a juice box. Have a nap. Go on."

He gives equally short shrift to the two generic shirt-and-tie detectives who pull in and interrogate Jesse about young Brock, not waiting for his legal representation to arrive before commencing their inquiries.

Fortunately, Jesse, having been through the wringer before, is no novice like Badger. "What did you tell them?" asks Saul. "I told them they were a couple of dicks!" Jesse can answer, truthfully. Once again, Saul dismisses them from the room like a couple of dogs who have had their front paws on the kitchen table. "Now, up you go. Make like you respect the rule of law. Make like you have manners. Pick it up, follow your partner." And, of course, the lawmen have no option but to sigh and comply.

LOOKING AT JAIL TIME?

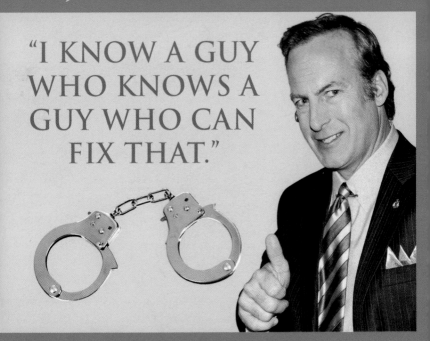

"I KNOW A GUY WHO KNOWS A GUY WHO CAN FIX THAT."

BETTERCALLSAUL.COM

Saul Goodman
ATTORNEY AT LAW

Agent Hank Schrader and Saul often cross paths at the police station. When they meet, each sledges the other like it's part of the ritual of law enforcement and revolving-door justice. "Your commercials? They suck ass," jeers Hank. "I've seen better acting in an epileptic whorehouse," he adds. "Is that like the one your mom works at?" Saul shoots back. "Is she still offering the two-for-one discount?" Boom. It's their version of pleasantries, momentarily brightening up the day with some cathartic smack talk before getting down to business.

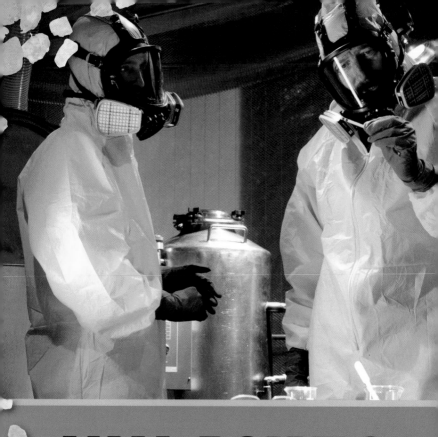

ANAL POLYPS
Handling Difficult Clients

Yeah? Well, Clarence Darrow never had a client like you!" exclaims Saul, when Walt compares him adversely to one of America's most famous and respected lawyers. It's true, the more remarkably so since Clarence Darrow represented Leopold and Loeb, who doubtless didn't cause him half the problems Walt and Jesse present to Saul. How much easier life could have been if they simply proceeded quietly and calmly with their meth business, keeping their heads down and earning Saul his steady percentage. But no: they had to bring to the table their volcanic personal issues, disaster-prone antics and inability to get on with or without the other. Worst of all, they constantly threaten to drag Saul into their ever-bubbling cauldron of danger. He may love their product, but he has serious doubts about their business acumen. "You two suck at peddling meth. Period. I'm amazed you got this far."

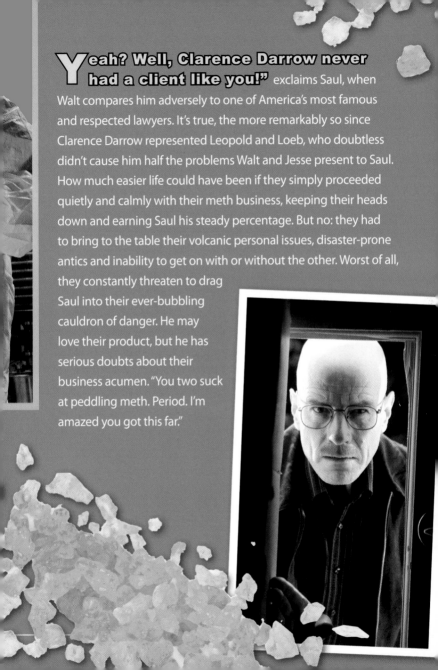

Jesse is the one who recommended Saul to Walt, after Saul was able to get his friend Emilio out of hot water, twice. "Dude's like Houdini!" Maybe in the old days, Jesse would have been an ideal client for Saul: daft and young enough to get into trouble, but sufficiently out of his depth enough that he would do as he was told. But now, Jesse's got attitude. He's all "Yo"s and tantrums. He's on and off drugs, and apt to respond to Saul's sound and urgent legal advice with a glassy-eyed, passive-aggressive "Whatever."

Trouble is, as time goes on, Jesse develops the most inconvenient of things: a conscience. When Jesse starts aimlessly driving around throwing thousands of dollars out of his car window, Saul interprets the charitable gesture as a glaring warning sign. When Jesse wants to leave his money to Kaylee Ehrmantraut after her grandfather Mike's sudden disappearance, Saul puts his foot down. "You got a guilty conscience? Visit the house of worship of your choice. But with all due respect, this ain't gonna fly." The cops are watching Kaylee, and no good deed is worth getting pinched over.

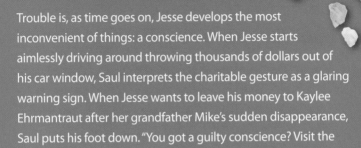

As for Walt, well, he truly is a pain. He's up his own reckless, hypocritical ass with condescension, unwilling to believe he's been forced to consort with a ludicrous lawyer like Saul—but constantly hitting him up for help all the same. Saul must adopt a concerned face while Walt embarks on lengthy rants about his latest round of troubles, and even keep a straight face when Walt complains about being "sucker punched" by Mike. Walt's the Maestro, the cooking genius, a high-risk client who needs the deluxe treatment— Saul has to cater to his needs as much as he can, despite the hubristic baggage that Walt carries with him. That goes for Jesse as well. It's too much, and as the heat gets way too hot, Saul vents his feelings generously: "If you two want to stick your wangs in a hornet's nest, it's a free country, but how come I always gotta get sloppy seconds, huh?" And then, the coup de grace: "If I ever get anal polyps, I'll know what to name them."

"IF I EVER GET
ANAL POLYPS,
I'LL KNOW WHAT
TO NAME THEM."

Saul Goodman

"THE PAIN IS PROFOUND—AND, BELIEVE ME, THE SETTLEMENT WILL BE PROFOUND"

Turning Disaster into Opportunity

When the commercial airliner Wayfarer 515 collides with another plane high above Albuquerque, thanks to a lapse in concentration on the part of the air-traffic controller father of Jesse's late girlfriend (who Walt let die), it is a harrowing sight. The explosion, in broad daylight, sends debris flying across the skies and adds 167 more to the toll of those who have lost their lives in connection to Walt's criminal enterprise. It's a dreadful, spectacular illustration of the consequences of bad actions, the remorse for which Walt must endure and try to deflect in order to carry on. For Saul, however, what the explosion yields is not eyeless teddy bears in swimming pools or body parts shattering windshields, but rather legal manna from heaven.

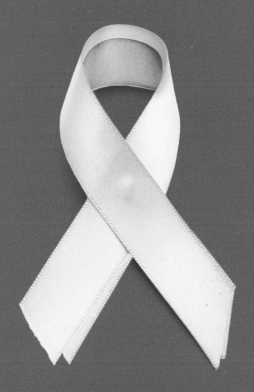

To the public eye, no one is more visibly heartbroken about the tragedy than Saul, who wears his blue ribbon in tribute to the deceased for months after it is truly necessary, like wearing white long after Labor Day. Whereas Walt clumsily attempts to assuage his guilt by downplaying the accident at a school assembly to the embarrassment of all, Saul unabashedly takes to TV-land to seek out justice for those on the ground who may have been affected by the disaster.

On his website, he prefaces his offer to the public to help them acquire redress with the simple slogan, "We're All Victims" set against the backdrop of a sad-looking American eagle. Men, women, and innocent children lost their lives, asserts Saul, before raising the "deep questions" posed by a tragedy like this. "Is there a God? How could he let this happen? Who did this to me?" and most important, "Who can I sue?"

"Did falling debris or body parts hit your home?? Car?? Place of business??" Saul does not skimp on the question marks at this time of sorrow. Maybe you or a loved one lost potential income now or in a possible future? Further ailments you might have suffered include nausea, survivor's guilt, or achy balls. All of these, Saul assures us—a tear running down the side of his face as he clutches a candle in tribute—are actionable. Better call Saul.

We hear him elaborate further over the phone to a potential client. "Did any little piece fall on your property? I'm not looking for a whole wing, just a nut, a bolt, a bag of peanuts, just as long as it caused you pain and suffering." Disasters like the Wayfarer 515 mid-air collision are mercifully rare—once in a lifetime, even. Which makes it all the more imperative for a guy like Saul to grab the opportunities they present with both hands. To fail to do so would make him unworthy of the term "attorney-at-law."

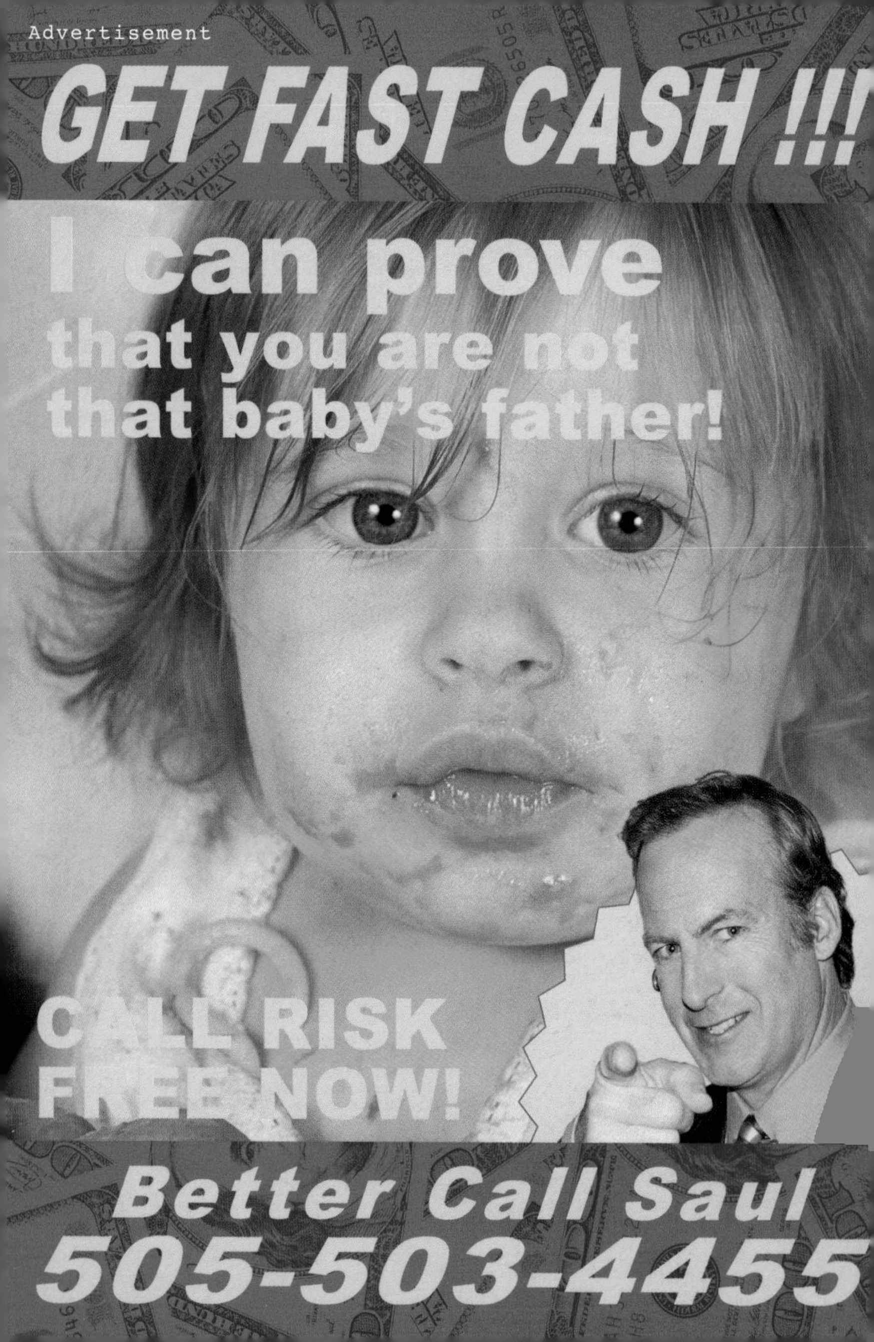
Advertisement
GET FAST CASH !!!
I can prove
that you are not
that baby's father!
CALL RISK
FREE NOW!
Better Call Saul
505-503-4455

THE LONE WOLF

Despite his relentlessly chipper spiel, despite all the guys he knows and the guys they know, Saul is a man alone in this world. We never see him interact with any friends or loved ones, and while we can wonder what or whom Saul goes home to after a long day defending the not-so innocent, there seem to be no painful conversations or tearful goodbyes when it comes time for him to disappear. Leaving his life behind only requires two blue suitcases and a new Nebraska driver's license with an unfamiliar name printed on it. Still, as he says to Jesse while attempting to get the hell out of Dodge, "When Walt tells me your employer took him out to the desert and threatened to murder his entire family, I sit up and take notice—because what am I, if not family?" How touching.

WORLD'S GREATEST ESTATE AGENT

Do You Concur?

With the vast array of services he provides his clients, it's amazing that Saul always appears so chipper. He must receive chemical assistance in some form, whether it be caffeine or something stronger, since it must be impossible for him to get a full night's rest. After working the usual nine to five providing standard legal services like criminal defense and filing lawsuits, Saul has to put in extra time facilitating his client's illegal enterprises—and crime does not follow bankers' hours. It's therefore more impressive when he goes above and beyond to help Jesse buy back the house his parents had kicked him out of after discovering the meth lab in the basement.

Like all respectable middle-class types, nothing thrills Mr. and Mrs. Pinkman more than the prospect of making money through real estate. When they sit down with Saul on his anonymous client's behalf and he makes a cash offer to purchase the house they've remodeled, their eyes naturally dance with glee. They had hoped such an offer might come from a more reputable practitioner of the law, but they're willing to put that aside once they find out the money is real. However, their lawyer is openly disdainful of Saul, whom he clearly regards as a clown.

It's when Saul brings up the small "hair in the soup," the matter of the price, that he shows his mettle. They want $875K; Saul offers $400K. Protesting that they spent nearly that much on the renovations alone, the Pinkmans and their lawyer get up to leave—at which point, Saul casually tosses in his grenade: the small matter of that basement meth lab, which they failed to disclose. Now, says Saul affably, he applauds the Pinkmans' "cojones" in trying to sneak a meth-contaminated property on to the market; he could issue criminal proceedings against them for doing so, but he suggests they simply accept the $400K and have everyone move quietly on with their lives. "How about it, counselor?" he asks, fixing his eyes on the condescending opposing counsel. "Do you concur?"

Mr. and Mrs. Pinkman may have cojones, but they're firmly in Saul's grip. Who would not want this man on their side in today's no-holds-barred real estate market?

A LAWYER FOR THE MODERN AGE

Saul's Website

It would be a shame not to give proper attention to Saul's Internet presence, www.bettercallsaul.com. "The law can be slippery!" says Saul, handling a giant, plastic fish by way of a prop on his website. "Let me handle it for you!" The site includes impressive testimonials from satisfied clients—including Badger, who gives a selective account of his arrest and credits Saul with his subsequent release; Carl, a local businessman who ensured his wife got nothing after their divorce thanks to Saul; and meth hooker Wendy ("I think I, like, owe him some money but he said we'd work it out"). The website comes from the same creative well that inspired his commercials and fashion choices, and it's sure to attract the attention of any poor soul with an arrest warrant and an Internet connection.